This Book is The Story of

Dear Grandma,

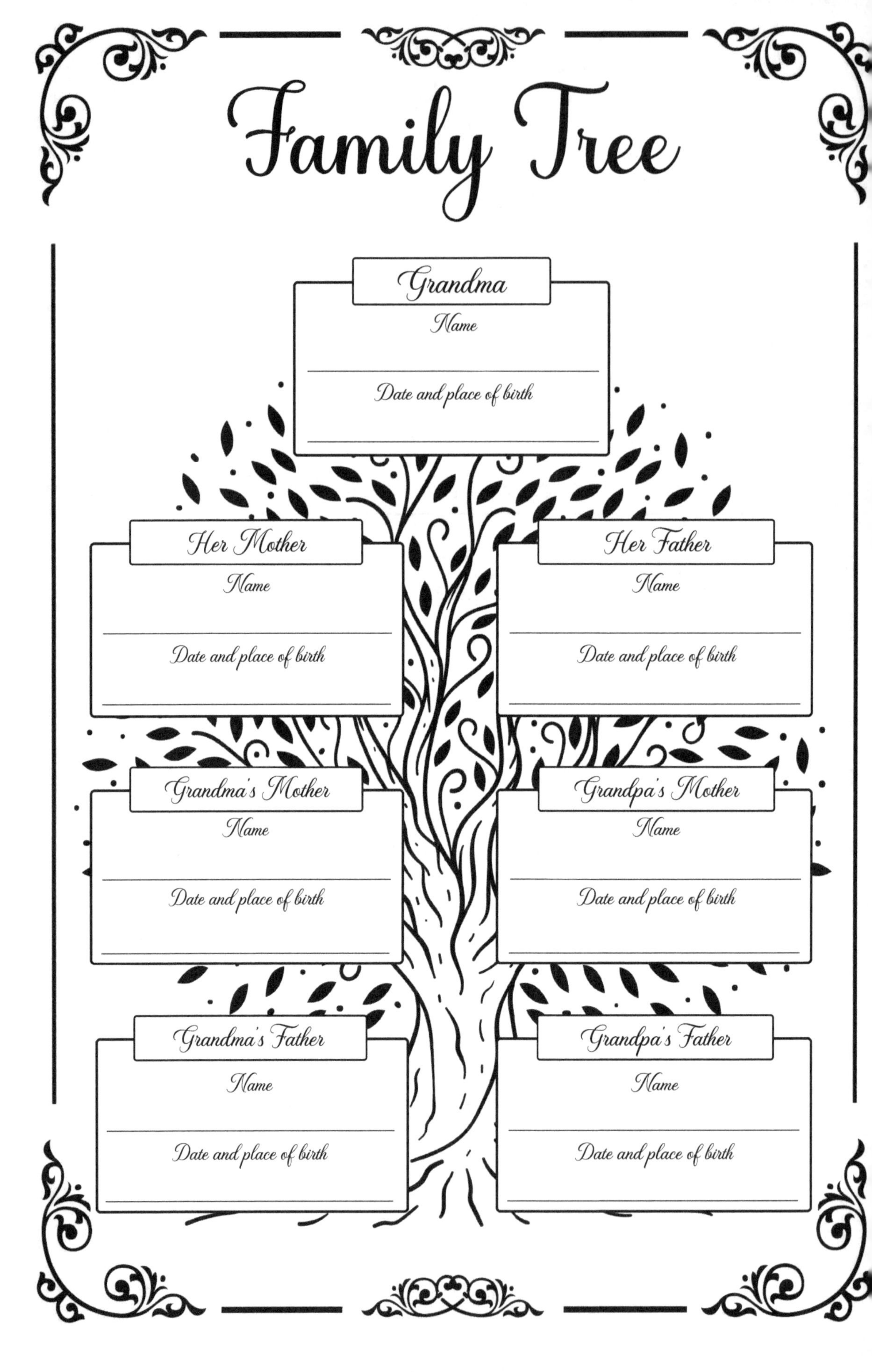

Family Tree
Grandma
Name
Date and place of birth
Her Mother
Name
Date and place of birth
Her Father
Name
Date and place of birth
Grandma's Mother
Name
Date and place of birth
Grandpa's Mother
Name
Date and place of birth
Grandma's Father
Name
Date and place of birth
Grandpa's Father
Name
Date and place of birth

Birth

'' Living with the birth of a child is our most accessible chance to grasp the meaning of the word miracle ''

Paul Clavel

WHEN AND WHERE WERE YOU BORN ?

WHAT IS YOUR FULL NAME ?

WAS YOUR BIRTH RELIGIOUSLY CELEBRATED ?

HOW OLD WERE YOUR PARENTS WHEN YOU WERE BORN ?

Childhood

> " Childhood is practically the most beautiful part of a person's life, the most innocent too "

CAN YOU DESCRIBE YOUR HOME, YOUR NEIGHBORHOOD AND THE CITY WHERE YOU GREW UP ?

HOW WAS YOUR CHILDHOOD ?

DID YOU HAVE A NICKNAME WHEN YOU WERE A KID ?
IF SO, WHAT WAS THAT NICKNAME AND WHAT WAS
THE REASON FOR IT ?

WHAT WERE YOUR FAVORITE TOYS ?

WHAT WERE YOUR FAVORITE GAMES ?

WHAT WAS YOUR FAVORITE TELEVISION SHOW AS A CHILD ?

DID YOU HAVE PETS ? WHAT WERE YOUR PET'S NAMES ?

WHAT WAS YOUR DREAM JOB WHEN YOU WERE A CHILD ?

WHO WAS THE OLDEST PERSON YOU REMEMBER ?

TELL ME ABOUT A TYPICAL DAY IN YOUR CHILDHOOD.

WHAT DIFFICULTIES DID YOU ENCOUNTER GROWING UP ?

HOW WAS THE WORLD DIFFERENT WHEN YOU WERE A CHILD ?

Family

"The family is one of nature's masterpieces"

George Santayana

TELL ME ABOUT YOUR FATHER (HIS NAME, DATE OF BIRTH, PLACE OF BIRTH, HIS PARENTS, ETC.)

CAN YOU SHARE WITH ME SOME MEMORIES YOU HAVE OF YOUR FATHER ?

TELL ME ABOUT YOUR MOTHER (HER NAMES, DATE
AND PLACE OF BIRTH, HER PARENTS, ETC.)

CAN YOU SHARE WITH ME SOME MEMORIES YOU HAVE OF YOUR MOTHER ?

TELL ME SOME MEMORIES YOU HAVE OF YOUR GRANDPARENTS.

WHAT ARE THE FULL NAMES OF YOUR SIBLINGS ?

TELL ME A STORY OR MEMORY ABOUT YOUR SIBLINGS ?

WHAT WERE YOUR FAMILY'S HOBBIES WHEN YOU WERE A CHILD ?

WHAT THREE WORDS COME TO MIND TO DESCRIBE OUR BIG FAMILY ?

DID YOUR FAMILY HAVE A PARTICULAR WAY OF CELEBRATING CERTAIN HOLIDAYS ?

ARE THERE TWO OR THREE DISHES THAT YOUR MOM OR DAD MADE, THAT MAKE YOU SMILE EVERY TIME YOU THINK ABOUT IT ?

WHAT DIFFICULTIES OR TRAGEDIES DID YOUR FAMILY EXPERIENCE WHEN YOU WERE YOUNG ?

Friendship

" A friend is someone who understands your past, believes in your future, and accepts you just the way " you are

Unknown

HOW DID YOU MEET YOUR BEST FRIEND ?

WHAT DID YOU AND YOUR BEST FRIEND LOVE TO DO TOGETHER ?

WAS THERE A CERTAIN PLACE YOU AND YOUR FRIENDS LIKED TO HANG OUT ?

HOW DID YOU MAKE FRIENDS AS AN ADULT ? WHAT DID YOU LIKE TO DO TOGETHER ?

WHAT'S ONE OF YOUR FAVORITE MEMORIES WITH A FRIEND ?

Travel

"The world is a book and those who do not travel read only a page"

Saint Augustine

WHICH COUNTRIES HAVE YOU TRAVELED TO ?

WHAT WAS YOUR BEST FAMILY VACATION ?

WHERE IS YOUR FAVORITE PLACE YOU'VE VISITED ? WHY ?

WHAT WAS THE MOST INTERESTING OR UNIQUE FOOD OR DISH YOU HAD WHILE TRAVELING ?

IF YOU COULD VISIT ANY PLACE YOU'VE ALREADY TRAVELED AGAIN, WHERE WOULD IT BE ? WHY ?

Education

" Education is the passport to the future, for tomorrow belongs to those who prepare for it today "

Malcolm X

WHAT TYPES OF BOOKS DO YOU LIKE TO READ ?

WHAT SCHOOL DID YOU GO TO AND WHERE WAS IT ?

HOW DID YOU EXPERIENCE THE SCHOOL YEARS ?

WHAT WAS YOUR FAVORITE SUBJECT IN SCHOOL ? WHY ?

HOW DID YOU BEHAVE AT SCHOOL ?

DID YOU HAVE FAVORITE TEACHERS ? WHY ?

WHAT IS YOUR FAVORITE MEMORY FROM SCHOOL ?

HOW WERE YOU DRESSED AT SCHOOL ?

WHAT SPORTS DID YOU PLAY AT SCHOOL ?

DID YOU RECEIVE ANY PRIZES FOR STUDIES OR ACTIVITIES AT SCHOOL ?

IF YOU WENT TO COLLEGE OR TOOK VOCATIONAL TRAINING, WHAT SCHOOL DID YOU GO TO ? WHAT DID YOU STUDY ? WHAT MEMORIES DO YOU HAVE FROM THOSE YEARS ?

WHO WERE YOUR FRIENDS AT SCHOOL ?
HOW WERE THEY ? WHAT HAPPENED TO THEM ?

Career

" Choose a job you love,
and you will never have
to work a day in
your life "

Confucius

WHAT WAS YOUR FIRST JOB ?

HOW DID YOU CHOOSE YOUR JOB ?

WHAT JOBS HAVE YOU HAD IN YOUR LIFE ? WHAT
MEMORABLE EXPERIENCES DO YOU KEEP FROM THEM ?

HOW OLD WERE YOU WHEN YOU RETIRED ?

WHO WAS ONE OF YOUR BIGGEST MENTORS ?

DO YOU HAVE ANY JOB ADVICE FOR ME WHEN I START WORKING ?

Adulthood

" The great challenge of adulthood is holding on to your idealism after you lose your innocence "

Bruce Springsteen

DID YOU HAVE A NICKNAME AS AN ADULT ?

IS THERE A FASHION THAT YOU PARTICULARLY LIKED ?

WHAT YOUNG ADULT HAVE YOU BEEN ?

HOW OLD WERE YOU WHEN YOU STARTED GOING OUT AT NIGHT ?

HAVE YOU EVER WON AN AWARD IN YOUR ADULT LIFE ?

WHAT ACTIVITIES DID YOU ENJOY DOING AS AN ADULT ?

Romantic Relationships

"You meet thousands of people and none of them really touch you. And then you meet one person and your life is changed forever"

DO YOU REMEMBER YOUR FIRST DATE ?

WHEN AND WHERE DID YOU MEET YOUR CURRENT PARTNER ?

HOW LONG HAD YOU KNOWN EACH OTHER WHEN YOU GOT MARRIED ?

HOW DID YOUR MARRIAGE PROPOSAL GO ?

WHEN AND WHERE DID YOU GET MARRIED ?

WHO WERE PRESENT AT YOUR WEDDING ?
(WITNESSES, BRIDESMAIDS, GUESTS, ETC.)

CAN YOU DESCRIBE TO ME THE DAY OF YOUR WEDDING ?

HOW WOULD YOU DESCRIBE YOUR PARTNER ?

WHAT DO YOU ADMIRE MOST ABOUT YOUR PARTNER ?

WHAT ADVICE WOULD YOU GIVE TO A CHILD OR GRANDCHILDREN ON THEIR WEDDING DAY ?

Motherhood

"Being a mother is learning about strengths you didn't know you had and dealing with fears you never knew existed"

Linda Wooten

HOW DID YOU FEEL WHEN YOU FOUND OUT YOU WERE GOING TO BE A PARENT FOR THE FIRST TIME?

HOW MANY CHILDREN DO YOU HAVE ? WHAT ARE
THEIR FIRST NAMES, DATES OF BIRTH AND WHERE
DO THEY CURRENTLY LIVE ?

TELL ME SOME MEMORIES ABOUT EACH OF YOUR CHILDREN.

WHAT IS ONE OF THE FUNNIEST THINGS YOUR KIDS DID ?

WHAT WAS THE MOST ENJOYABLE PART OF YOUR CHILDREN'S EDUCATION FOR YOU ?

IF YOU HAD TO START OVER, WHAT WOULD YOU CHANGE ABOUT THE WAY YOU RAISED YOUR CHILDREN ?

WHAT WAS THE HARDEST PART ABOUT RAISING YOUR CHILDREN ?

WHAT HAS BEEN THE MOST REWARDING THING ABOUT BEING A PARENT ?

WHAT ADVICE WOULD YOU GIVE YOUR CHILDREN AND GRANDCHILDREN TO BE A GOOD PARENT ?

WHAT DO YOU LIKE ABOUT YOUR ROLE AS A GRANDMOTHER ?

Generally

"Three things in life :
your health, your mission,
and the people you love.
That's it"

Naval Ravikant

WHAT IS THE MOST DIFFICULT THING YOU HAVE EXPERIENCED ?

WHAT IS THE MOST AMAZING THING THAT YOU HAVE EXPERIENCED ?

WHO WERE YOUR MODELS AND YOUR INSPIRATIONS ?

HOW DO YOU FEEL ABOUT IMPORTANT DECISIONS IN YOUR LIFE, SUCH AS YOUR PROFESSION, YOUR STUDIES AND YOUR SPOUSE ?

IF YOU COULD GO BACK AND START SOME THINGS OVER AGAIN, WHAT WOULD YOU CHANGE ?

WHAT ARE THE LIFE LESSONS THAT YOU WOULD LIKE TO PASS ON TO YOUR POSTERITY ?

WHAT'S THE FUNNIEST JOKE YOU KNOW ?

WHAT TALENTS DO YOU HAVE ? HOW DID YOU FIND
THEM OUT ? WHAT HAVE YOU DONE TO CULTIVATE AND
IMPROVE THEM ?

WHAT PERSONAL VALUES ARE VERY IMPORTANT TO YOU ? WHAT HAVE YOU DONE (OR ARE YOU DOING NOW) TO TEACH THESE VALUES TO YOUR CHILDREN ?

WHAT DO YOU THINK ARE THE BEST INVENTIONS SINCE YOU WERE BORN ?

LIST INTERESTING THINGS THAT YOU HAVE EXPERIENCED IN YOUR LIFE.

WHAT ARE THE THINGS THAT MAKE YOU HAPPY IN YOUR LIFE ?

THINKING OF PEOPLE FROM ALL OVER THE WORLD AND FROM ALL TIMES, LIST THE NAMES OF FIVE PEOPLE WHO YOU CONSIDER TO BE GREAT MEN OR WOMEN. WHAT DID THEY DO THAT WAS GREAT TO YOU?

Pictures

&

Memories